Next Life

Wesleyan Poetry

Also by Rae Armantrout

POETRY

Up to Speed

Veil: New amd Selected Poems

The Pretext

Made to Seem

Necromance

Couverture

Precedence

The Invention of Hunger

Extremities

MEMOIR

True

Next Life

Rae Armantrout

Wesleyan University Press | *Middletown, Connecticut*

Published by Wesleyan University Press, Middletown, CT 06459
www.wesleyan.edu/wespress
© 2007 by Rae Armantrout
Printed in the United States of America

5 4 3 2 1

The author wants to thank the editors of the following journals and anthologies
where these poems have appeared: *Chicago Review, Conjunctions, Explosive,
Five Fingers Review, Jacket, Jubilat, Kiosk, Lit, Logopoeia, Mandorla, Mississippi
Review, No: A Journal of the Arts, Poetry Society of America Magazine, Shiny,
The Canary, The New Yorker, The Poker, Tolling Elves, Van Gogh's Ear, Verse, 88,
American Hybrid* (Norton, 2007), and *War and Peace* (O Press, 2004).

Library of Congress Cataloging-in-Publication Data
Armantrout, Rae, 1947–
 Next life / Rae Armantrout.
   p. cm. — (Wesleyan poetry)
 ISBN-13: 978–0–8195–6820–5 (alk. paper)
 ISBN-10: 0–8195–6820–1 (alk. paper)
 I. Title.
 PS3551.R455N49 2007
 811'54—dc22   2006024145

Contents

Next Life

Tease

For lack of which
we put ourselves
in a cop's place

as he puts himself
inside the head
of a serial killer rapist

who appears to be
teasing the police.

*

Bare tree
is to human skeleton

as the holy spirit
likens objects

briefly

to make the world up
of provisional pairs.

*

It makes sense
to turn that corner
in a black sedan

and to write down
everything that passes.

2 | To quick-step up the street
       in a knit red cap
       one time only.

       *

       Red cap is to
       one time only
       as

Line

A soul is like a line, then—
one-dimensional?

The other nouns suggest
that we extend our range.

Our division-head wants us
 to reverse-engineer the thing.

So to be scolded
is to be thoughtless,

and a thoughtless person
is a "diva,"

meaning someone
recognized by others,

someone who continues
to exist.

*

You're trying to draw the line
maybe,

"rooting around"
down there,

as we used to put it.

Where do these words come from

anyway?

Even the pit
is sick of itself by now,

has been calling itself
an "acid-hole"
for years.

The whole run-through
makes us queasy.

Reserved

A small dark room
behind each lid,
unoccupied. Reserved?

*

"The waiting room was different
this time," I said, warily,

as if someone might have tricked us
into believing
there was just one room

or that there were other times.

*

I'm waiting on a transfer
of poison

among strung leaves
through the Americas

by dictator, no,
dictation.

Or I'm going ahead.

Narrative prepares me
to see
whatever I see next.

*

Not getting lost
but looping
then extending myself

afresh,
starburst,

reversing myself
as if turning
to face a partner

Two, Three

Sad, fat boy in pirate hat.
Long, old, dented,
copper-colored Ford.

How many traits
must a thing have
in order to be singular?

(Echo persuades us
everything we say
has been said at least once

                   before.)

Two plump, bald men
in gray tee-shirts
and tan shorts

are walking a small bulldog—
followed by the eyes
of an invisible third person.

The Trinity was born
from what we know
of the bitter

symbiosis of couples.
Can we reduce echo's sadness
by synchronizing our speeches?

Is it the beginning or end
of *real* love
when we pity a person

because, in him,
we see ourselves?

As (2)

Consciousness entrenches itself by hijacking the orienting-response, forcing it to work overtime to produce a continuous present.

*

As keeps it coming,
keeps us company

to the same extent
that,

and at once,

in proportion

with clauses transposed.

*

Now's hopeful
pucker.

*

Three birds make
a framing gesture,

an inclusive sweep,

as the background
color's
drained and chilled

Blur

I'm called home
but don't go.

I have enough past
and future

to accompany me now.

The solitary one
interferes with itself.

They should give up
                counting

Close

As if a single scream
gave birth

to whole families
of traits

such as "flavor," "color,"
"spin"

and this tendency to cling.

2

Dry, white frazzle
in a blue vase—

beautiful—

a frozen swarm
of incommensurate wishes.

3

Slow, blue, stiff
are forms

of crowd behavior,

mass hysteria.

Come close.

The crowd is made of
little gods

and there is still
no heaven

Theory of Everything

It both hurtles
and fidgets,

otherwise
it's empty space?

*

A wide swath
of baby-talk—

blue
and feathery green,
I insisted,

swinging up,

but Mother
was no longer playing.

*

Everything that stays
once meaning has cleared out

is *true?*

*

Tomorrow
the sun eats the earth,

14 | now
so many leaves are new,

not asking
to be recognized.

Thing

We love our cat
for her self
regard is assiduous
and bland,

for she sits in the small
patch of sun on our rug
and licks her claws
from all angles

and it is far
superior
to "balanced reporting"

though, of course,
it is also
the very same thing.

Empty

The present
must be kept empty
so that anything
can happen:

> The Queen of England visits
> Amanda's hot tub

> as a prophylaxis?·

a discrepancy
between one's view of things
and what comes to pass.

*

It's ironic when something
has a meaning to someone

> "Gotta go
> Gotta go
> Gotta go
> right now"

other than that
intended by the speaker.

> sings the bladder-control model
> from the fidgety TV
> above the dying woman's bed.

It's ironic when a set
contains no elements.

*Of a person, frivolous.
Of a body, shrunken.*

The Subject

It's as if we've just been turned human
in order to learn
that the beetle we've caught
and are now devouring
is our elder brother
and that we
are a young prince.

*

I was just going to click
on "Phoebe is changed
into a mermaid
tomorrow!" when suddenly
it all changed
into the image
of a Citizen watch.

*

If each moment is in love
with its image
in the mirror of
adjacent moments

(as if matter stuttered),

then, of course, we're restless!

"What is a surface?"
we ask,

trying to change the subject.

Units

Being a threesome

of young palms,
a triangle
containing dusk,

a doubled
reflection which might yet
be redoubled,

is a way of being
one
by being numbered

so as to have not
begun again

oblivious,

in excess

A Distance

I'm confined to a wheelchair and spend my time
doing small oil paintings.

I'm 11 and would like photos
of nature at its best.

I'm looking for milk bottles.

I used to collect red
Jerusalem artichokes.

I want to weave small rugs on a loom.

I find myself with a long cape
such as a bullfighter might use.

I'd like to be the misunderstood
monster

who's only a boy—

but am a woman,
aged 56.

*

A girl's doll is herself,
caught as if
unawares.

From a distance, she watches
the monster

approaching her bed.

With contempt.

But whose contempt is it?

Cursive

In my country,
in "Toy Story,"

sanity meant keeping
a set distance

between one's role
as a figurine
and one's "self-image."

This gap
was where the soul
was thought to live.

*

When he thought of suicide, he thought,

"It ends here!"

and

"Let's do it!"

As if a flying leap
were a form of camaraderie.

As if a cop and his
comic relief partner
faced off
against moguls.

Crossed wires released such
hope-like sparks.

*

This thing was called
"face of the deep,"

this intractable blank
with its restless cursive

The Ether

The room is ether-bright,
rigid,

adrift in words

or I am

an afterthought,
refusing to dissolve.

Nothing

to be taken away;
to be added.

*

What can words say?

Chaplain-service at the checkout;

a desire
to be credible
across the straight.

A man and woman
finish sentences
and laugh.

Each sentence is both
an acquiescence
and a dismissal.

Agreement

"That's a nice red," you said,
but now the world was different

so that I agreed

with a puzzled
or sentimental certainty

as if clairvoyance
could be extended to the past.

And why not?

With a model sailing ship
in the window
of a small, neat house

and with a statuette
of a stable boy
on the porch,
holding a lamp up

someone was making something clear—

perhaps that motion
is a real character.

2

How *should* we feel

about "the eraser?"

"Rampages" wears one expression
while "frantically" wears another:

conjoined twins,
miraculously separated
on Judgment Day?

Then "only nothingness"
is a bit vague.

But words are more precise than sight—
increasingly!

3

The very old man shuffles very slowly
not between
the white lines of a crosswalk
but down one of them.

Like a figure in a dream,
his relation to meaning
is ominous

Away

The boy and girl leave
the tired woman behind
gladly.

They are off
to find their real mother,

she of the golden
edible house, the
cunning hunger.

*

From your snort of recognition
I can tell

that you are the baby
crocodile,

adrift
on a floating mat
of papyrus.

In your yellow, crescent eye
an insouciant attention.

*

Yellow flecks
of glitter
in the cement—

28 | clusters?—

each a faraway
answer

to an ill-posed problem.

Reversible

Try this.

Shadows of leaves
between shadows of venetian blinds

bounce

like holes

across the scroll of a
player-piano.

But are similes reversible?

Try this.

Trunk of a palm tree
as the leg

of a one-legged
ballerina.

2

That's a bad
Sean Connery, but
a good Prince.

We wake up to an empty room
addressing itself in scare quotes.

"Happen" and "now"
have been smuggled out,

to arrive safely in the past tense.

We come home to a cat
made entirely of fish.

Headline Song

Bush vows victory
over terror.

For the orphans,
nightmare lasts.

We'll hang on
to what proved useful.

Eggs are full
of flame retardant.

Clear

An old woman is being led through the parking lot by two girls. They hold her hands and speak in energetic, explanatory bursts while she cranks her head this way and that as if expecting something which has yet to appear.

As if the crystalline clarity of this ocean pool, cradled in two lava arms, meant something which we had been waiting to hear, something indistinguishable from meaning itself, and unchanging, so that, finally, it's we who turn to go.

Echo

See how
confusion can produce it—

the transfiguration.

Your future dressed up
as one

echoed, "Aha!"

*

The street pales
to the same shapes
as before:

tree trunks, buildings, parked cars.

The whole spectral hard-on
quite literally repulsive!

You can never touch it

and really
you wouldn't want to.

Yonder

1

Anything cancels
everything out.

If each point
is a singularity,

thrusting all else
aside for good,

"good" takes the form
of a throng
of empty chairs.

Or it's ants
swarming a bone.

2

I'm afraid
I don't love
my mother
who's dead

though I once—
what does "once" mean?—
did love her.

So who'll meet me over yonder?
I don't recognize the place names.

Or I do, but they come
from televised wars.

Us

Your stylized expectancy,
grown old,

still head-cocking at newcomers.

Car called Echo;
car called Mirage—

there's no one like you.

Your sparrow-like uptick
with the black pinpoint

dead center.
That's where I'm sitting.

Violin reiterations,

clockwork kicks
in the nothing-doing,

still passing for pleasure.

2

Now I'm with you
and we're looking for you.

You've left a note saying
you've gone into hiding

because they're onto you.

We drive down this street
pointing out buildings
where you might be holed up

though it's clear that they
could be following us

Our Daphne

If resemblance
is the passage

down which meaning flees,

branching
now and now,

some guy's
carved a climbing vine

in wood

meaning,
"I'd

follow you
anywhere"

Visits

Thomas puts his hand
into the open wound

between conception and object:
the local

news reports an escondido woman
has filled her home

with "upwards of a thousand
statuettes

of Lady Liberty."

It is from this wound
that humans first emerged.

Many believe
that authorities conspire
to convince them

they are each
alone—

and are not being
visited.

That an orifice
is not being probed
by mysterious intention.

As if
these narrow,
shady steps

lined with well-trimmed bushes

lead nowhere

Parse

1

Backwash of revelation:

to see these articulated,
new weeds
as one thing;

to hear bird-chirps
parse the plenum.

2

When aren't
we synonymous with
increased vigilance,

now with *this time*,
now *in this sense?*

3

Tongues tapping
the roofs

of our own mouths
to make meaning.

4

Then God diddles us
with this sunset,

its pale pinks and
tender blues. This

one-two rinse
reminds us of something,

if only our own
depth-of-feeling

Soon

With me always

eclipsed-he-or-she's
soon
to be evoked.

We live by faith
alone.

*

I want to tell you
midges
rise from spring grasses.

*

Shining path
around lifted, tattered fronds,

silence around
the sound of the saw

Framing

What you won't see today:

juniper's tough skein.

*

The rolling
hummocks

have grown syntax—

tassels and bells—

for careless
wings to be among.

*

The tic
in articulation.

*

The present is cupped

by a small effort
of focus—

its muscular surround.

You're left out.

Short Story

"The houses down there are all bunched up," she tells the
young man in the seat beside her.

As the runway nears, she raises and lowers one closed hand
and says, "Ba-bump!" to indicate she knows what's coming.

Afterwards, she adds, "Scary moment," though no one looks
frightened. The young man nods, perhaps to acknowledge the
authority with which even ordinary events address us,

perhaps in deference to the woman's wish to circumscribe a
version so it can be handled, touched,

although
if this is the evidence

Promise

Canary yellow of the school bus;
school bus yellow of the SUV.

2

I was thinking that the saying
"I'll sleep when I'm dead"
is dead wrong.
But then accuracy
is a moot point
in this context. Moot points
exude a certain charm—
although the transition
from mattering to not
is generally quite painful.

Then we broke through the cloud cover
and I saw what I called
a bracelet
of yellowish lights
extended over water.
Headlights of cars
on a bridge, as it turned out.
And still beckoning.
A promise that can only be kept
by being made and made again

Continuity

It dawns blind.

It resets automatically.

To metabolism and panic.

It comes forward.

I am only

my mother.

*

It restarts automatically
as a zombie flick
to remind us

that hunger waits outside
all reason.

It's after us
and before us—always

trying to get "in."

*

The bits we can't think of now

are jealous.

They push forward,

seamlessly, so

not existing

as they won't

after

In Part

48 | "Pray to Persephone,

Dread Queen
of being changed totally."

*

The gods specialized back then
the way
one part of the brain
controls the hands
while another controls crying.

One says this in a dream
which is really a speech
she receives an award for
as she gives it.

*

Resting briefly
in the form
as given:

three doves
on a high-rise ledge.

Everything sparkles and
then doesn't.

What can description do?

The dream—a froth
of syllables and lights.
A lost
girl, cross
section of a girl,
who floats on the surface
tension between bed
rock
and rising

Pronouncements

Light was pronouncing

rectangle after rectangle

on a hardwood floor.

*

In the same way that a baby
learns to move her arms,

"Let"

led to "was"
and then back to "was."

Meaning—which one word
was unable to absorb—

splashed onto everything.

That's when humans were created—

those who confuse
intelligibility with purpose.

*

A Country, Aquarium, Signature, Paradise, Style Kabob
came out.

As planets and protons
invent themselves by spinning,

so a mind
turns on itself

in a body's dark space

Arrangements

The way the ancient
explosion
has arranged itself.

At the bus stop:

a hunched woman
        with sparse
auburn hair

above a Peter Pan
collar,

a blue jumper,
Mary Janes.

*

What novelty has
always promised:

claiming to,

first co-
        alesce.

Make cleave

un   to

        as
        almost
        as

Last scattering surface.

*

Variations
in air

pressure:

angel
voices

Remote

The breath coming
to rest

like a small frog
at the bottom of a fish tank,

then darting up to surface
now again,

is mine?

*

Remote and, by now, automated
distress calls fill the air.

*

Do you believe this?
Metaphor

shifts a small weight
there and back.

My self-reflection shames God
into watching

Incorporation

1

Casual at the checkout counter,
a man buys three kinds
of candy bar

and a pack of sausages.

2

Having arisen effortlessly
and without sensation,

the mind will seem
to haunt the organs.

3

Each viewer
is the solitary driver

trying to evade the commercial's
marching-band

but confronted
at each intersection
by his doppelganger,

a wild-eyed drum major
mad for this new car.

Your job
is to make the drum major
vanish.

Make It New

Shaking the parts of speech
like fluff
in a snow globe—

the way sleep scrambles
life's detritus.

Each poem says,
"I'm desperate"

then, "Everything
must go!"

(To hear something familiar here
leads to careful laughter.)

"Go" where?

The steady pressure
on the accelerator
can be stipulated
in advance

as can the stubby bushes
blurred in peripheral vision.

And someone will have set down
a diner or a gas station
at a desolate crossroads

and tried naming it
to evoke

the whole human situation

while
satirizing
the impulse to do so.

What that name will be
is the one thing we don't know

Some

Someone insists on forming sentences
on my pillow
when all I want is sleep:

marching orders,
wisecracks about others elsewhere.

I'd like to kill her
but I'm told it's she

who must go on
at all cost.

*

The old cat casts her eye
about the carpet near her,
jerkily,
preparing to lick herself.

*

A sense of mission   lost
in ink's
jagged outcrops.

I was trying to tell myself
what I must have known
before

in a form
I wouldn't recognize at first.

*

Blinksmanship.

Bright ranks of
                of

slip rapidly
over bars of it.

Blank-pedaling.

Long live illumined
oblongs

with this shuttling
                cross-hatch

Passing

Wrapped strands and

what passes
                    for messages,

what pulls itself
                    apart to flash,

the twinkle
or tickle
of articulation,

counting its own
"t"s and "s"s,

to pretend, "This way!"
                    and that,

to be between
the mass-produced
                    glass ball reflections

Shine On

If every expression
outlives its origin

*

The seemingly decorative white
trim around each
ruffled coleus leaf

is not to be trusted?

*

In the last analysis,
at the Planck length,

the energy required
to ask the right question
is so great

that inquiry itself forms
a miniature black hole.

Space may be imagined
as a kind of foam
pocked with such erasures,

interlocking scribble-throughs.

*

A smile torn in a pumpkin,

now grossly inflated,

sits atop the Spirit
Super-Store

Again

General Foods ads from the '50s line a restaurant's walls.
It's not nostalgic; nostalgia requires a place
to which we might want to go back.

It's our felt distance
from the supposed past
as collectible,

our credulities and
incredulities
as collectibles.

The sketchier the better, the way
a simply drawn young mother

pours milk from a pitcher
onto Corn Flakes

for a Cool Start

and the compressed
airiness
of Rice Krispies.

2

The static seems jumpy tonight,
anxious, randomized, but

perhaps not truly random.

64 | That's what worries some of us.

Hollywood itself

tells us the background
is composed of voices

speaking from beyond
their own annihilation.

We ought to be frightened
of the reconstituted

pronominal fizz
that invades us,

the wavery, weasely persistence

which, once we start to listen,
demands to be heard

Seed

The presence of a partner
incites rehearsal.

Oh yeah, oh yeah, and

The noncoding end
becomes a target.

Oh yeah, oh yeah, and

Each one competes
to remind the other

of an episode
(oh yeah)

from a film that
both have seen.

*

Odd that an equation
describing a relationship

could be solved
by a echo:

"33."

*

Tired, you slip

into belief, into

dream with its immediate
branches.

The familiar sense
of growing up

from seed

takes you back
and in

Ins and Outs

The "necessary fiction" that, if I live inside you, and you're part
of me, we're spread safely thin.

Gauzy.

Are you defiantly
frilly?

Evasively frilly?

Forgetfully frilly?

You're brilliantly ragged
in this aquarium light,

in your "getting-somewhere"
costume,

your red ins-and-outs
rippling.

For the meanwhile.

In the time-being

Resting

1

The blather of rival versions,
small claims,

that the television
judges sweep away

for my sake

to arrive
at the simple

2

If I stand still,

"now"
both gathers

and relaxes shoreward—
pent-up, permissive.

If I can stare
without blinking

State

Spring's simple Kleenex clumps
of cloud

as before.

What was I promised?

An Earth both clockwork
and cherub?

*

I walk back to the couch
in time's

slo-mo coronal blow-off
                    weather.

*

This scene presents me
walking on an interstate,
barefoot,

thinking it's strange
that I'm not tired at all.

*

It's about
"making a statement."

The screen is made of jitters
known as iterations,

differing in charge and
orbital spin.

I've been practicing

Yoohoo

Sun lights up a pelt
of dust on the receiver.

Being unexpected,
this is a kind of call.

Cross names out
and things are all made up

of contrary, percussive,
adjectival tugs.

I remember someone
wrestled an angel,

                    a signal.

*

The present's chronic
revision

which a poem
reenacts.

The open vowel
(peek-a-boo)
pelvis

through which you
"came into this world"

sits on the shelf

in a mausoleum
now,

world on either side of it

Propensity

We learn that each
is eternal and identical except

as regards its wobble

and its exact propensity
for being elsewhere.

*

We are each perturbed

and hope to say so
first or best.

*

When we wish for anything,
we also wish

for time to pass.
From this

we can infer
that time and wish are one

substance
or that we have caused them

to become enmeshed.

*

Having enveloped a utility pole,
the morning glory gapes
in all directions.

Twizzle

He who finds a knot
in himself
where a soft expanse should be

will want to tell
the nearest person to him.

But this can be known
now

and lived later on

so the start of it
is always somewhere else.

*

Evenly hovering attention:
pocked concrete.

Long tangles of gray-
green eucalyptus leaves

twizzle,
throwing sharp shadows.

If I could just signal
so variously.

*

The trees upstart.

By "virgin"
we meant inaccessible
just now,

and by "inaccessible"
we meant original.

The virgin birth
can only happen once

everywhere

and doesn't dare stop

Next Life

1

Last of all and
most reluctantly
you said goodbye to
"near"
and "far away."

2

Fuzzy-minded
clouds sprout

from one another's
foreheads.

But you were more exact.

You unzipped yourself
in the dark

back there,

counted yourself
in half

and cut.

That was before numbers.

3

"Don't be a commodity;

be a concept:"

a ghostly configuration
of points or parts—

trivia snippets—

which appears inside
locked cabinets.

Be untraceable
but easy to replicate.

Be relative.

Be twice as far
and halfway back

ABOUT THE AUTHOR

Rae Armantrout is Professor of Poetry and Poetics at the University of California at San Diego. She is the author of eight books of poetry, most recently *Up to Speed* (Wesleyan, 2004), *Veil: New and Selected Poems* (Wesleyan, 2001), *The Pretext* (Green Integer, 2001), and *Made to Seem* (Sun and Moon, 1995). Armantrout's work has been included in many anthologies, including *The Oxford Book of American Poetry* (Oxford, 2006), *Poems for the New Millenium* (California, 1998), *Postmodern American Poetry: A Norton Anthology* (Norton, 1993), and Scribner's *Best American Poetry of 1988, 2001, 2002,* and *2004.*